The Ma

Drs. Willard and Karen Smith

A book of helpful points that will help you navigate marriage

Table of Content

Introduction

Chapter 1 A Prayer you're your marriage.......4

Chapter 2 Intimacy and Sex in Marriage……...6

Chapter 3 What is Sex...………………………...8

Chapter 4 There may be a spiritual ………10 reason why some marriages struggle

Chapter 5 How to accept your husband or... 15 Wife

Chapter 6 Putting some Fun into Marriage…..19 Marriage

Chapter 7 Acknowledge your partner………...23 their needs

Chapter 8 When you have had a bad………….26 moment with your husband or wife

Chapter 9 Being unequally yoked…...............33

Chapter 10 The Step-parent Issue……………..35

Chapter 11 Money and your marriage………..41

Chapter 12 The Importance of Marriage…….45

Chapter 13   Thinking about getting out.........50

INTRODUCTION

This book is written as a quick help aid, designed to help you navigate through the challenges of marriage. It contains reminders of things that will help you with different situations and with things that you may not have to consider as being part of the challenges in your marriage.

Read it with an open mind and follow the directives that many of the chapters present. There are no guarantees in this book, but the information has proven to work for hundreds of people worldwide.

We wish you the best of blessings in your marriage and we believe that with the help of God, you can have a bountiful marriage.

Drs. Will and Karen

Chapter 1
A Prayer for your marriage

Father, in the name of Jesus, I lift this marriage before your throne. Thank you for allowing them to be husband and wife in respect and honor of your commands. I pray that you would help them each understand your word and all that it says a husband and a wife should be to each other. I pray that pride, rebellion, offense, fault-finding, or even bitterness has no place in their marriage. I pray that love, peace, hope, joy for each other, prayer, and healing on every level covers them both. I pray that their children line up with your word and that the spirit of unity draws the family together. We speak, that there is no division in the family. We speak that all your favor is upon the husband, the wife, and the children. We break the works of the enemy in their lives and we speak your words only for them. We speak life in any dead situation. We speak healing of emotions, forgiveness, and unconditional love toward the other. Thank you, Lord, for renewing what the enemy tried to destroy. Thank you, Lord, for new revelations in the minds of the husband, wife, and children. We speak the words, " All is well!" In Jesus' name, we pray. Amen!

Chapter 2

Intimacy and Sex in Marriage

You cannot discuss marriage without involving these two. Is there a difference? Depending on who you ask, you may hear someone say that they are the same, but they are different; and often women, know that and complain to their men that what they need is not sex, but intimacy. To be fair, we need both at the proper time. The lack of these two can break a marriage up but include these in your marriage (no matter what your age) and you will see a difference. Let's talk about it:

WHAT IS INTIMACY?

People refer to "being intimate when they discuss sex. Although the two can be intertwined, intimacy goes beyond the physical act.

Intimacy involves emotional connection and trust that seeks to bring the couple closer. Sex brings a couple closer in its way, but intimacy is so much more than physical pleasure.

Intimacy allows each person to be vulnerable. You can expose your true feelings and share some of your deepest and most loving thoughts while simply holding the person's hand or even just lying next to them. There are three ways to be intimate with your partner.

The three ways to be intimate are:

- **emotional intimacy:** a deep feeling of closeness and trust
- **physical intimacy:** includes touching in a way that enhances feelings of closeness and desire
- **sexual intimacy:** combines the physical act of sex with emotional closeness and trust

Chapter 3

WHAT IS SEX?

In general, sex is the act of two people physically involved in the act itself. Sex does not have to be intimate. It may or may not involve transparency and expressions of the person's innermost feelings. It is an act with the objective being a physical pleasure. There are times when intimacy is involved, but more often than not, intimacy is not the main objective.

Again, sex may include intimacy, but it may not. What is important to know about sex in marriage is that it is important and that it does have benefits beyond pleasure. It is good for you emotionally and physically. Some couples will agree that sex has helped to create a connection with their partner. Some even say that it has health benefits and liken it to physical exercise similar to the benefits of walking.

Medical Science believes that during the process of orgasm, your body gives what feels like a natural high. It is at this time that endorphins, which are hormones that block pain are released and the feeling that is given makes the person(s) feel good.

It is also said that sex leads to great health in general, better sleep, better self-esteem, less stress, and even longer life.

Both sex and intimacy have their place in marriage. The important thing to remember is that no matter how young or old you are, sex has to be discussed between the two of you at some point and the idea of intimacy must be defined clearly for your partner to determine

how you see each.

Chapter 4

There may be a spiritual reason why some marriages struggle!

Have you ever considered that the very first attack on humankind was against marriage? Satan launched an all-out strategy to not only cause man to sin against God and His instructions, but one that could have created a divide between men and women throughout time. Through this attack, marriage between the two that God joined together could have ended, thus validating what we see today. I will be the first to admit that the grace of God has covered me from the act of divorce (under justified circumstances), but divorce is never the highest order of God. My point here is that we need to consider the spiritual side of things when it comes to marriage and the challenges that are faced. Sometimes, there is a Satanic plot behind the division of a man and a woman. Understand that not everything is caused by Satan, but we would be missing it, if we did not acknowledge that some things are.

Why would Satan try to divide a man and his wife (especially believers)? Consider the following:

There is evidence of the ontological equality of men and women as both were created in the *imago dei*. The first chapters of Genesis also reveal God's expectations for marriage: (1) Marriage is a heterosexual, (2) monogamous, (3) sexual, (4) and a patricentric relationship. Patricentrism means that the husband serves as the leading, protecting, and providing entity of the marriage and family. Marriage is also a permanent relationship. In our day and time, we know that divorce seems normal, but by design, marriage was meant to last forever. The phrase used by Adam to describe Eve ("bone of my bones and flesh of my flesh") was used to convey permanent blood/family relationships that could not be broken. Lastly, marriage is one flesh, covenantal relationship that creates a "corporate personality" through the sexual union of two unified spouses, one man, and one woman.

Tragically, this ideal was overturned by the rebellion against God. In Genesis 3, Satan enters the Garden of God to oppose his creator and deceive God's creation. What happened next set the blueprint for how Satan would attack marriage. He subtly comes in and attacks one or both and distracts them from the main objective of being together. From that point, he launches both external and internal accusations to divide the two up.

The good news is that God promised this conflict would end when his messiah would crush Satan's head and forever render him powerless. But until that time comes, we must understand that not all marriage issues are natural. Satan and his demonic forces are not yet totally subdued so Satan still "prowls around like a roaring lion, seeking someone to devour" (1 Pet 5:8). His target is the unity that is found in man, God's Church, and marriage.

Divorce became a part of the strategy to dissolve what God put His approval on. Satan causes distractions that lead to the lust of the flesh, the lust of the eye, and the pride of life.

You will be amazed at how many marriage issues are started by fear, doubt, unbelief, distrust, unforgiveness, bitterness, and so many more. All of these things come from Satan himself. God is our only answer and through prayer and His word, we can overcome the tools that Satan uses against marriage.

Chapter 5

How to accept your husband or wife

As you grow together in marriage, there is a gift that is worth seeking God for. It is called "ACCEPTANCE." You and Your Husband/Wife are different. Couples who have been married for a long time know what acceptance is because it is that thing that kept them together when they may have felt like giving up. It is difficult to accept your husband or wife, without the help of God and without wanting to love and understand them. No matter how long you have been married, you know that you are still finding things that you need to accept about your Husband or Wife.

Acceptance is key to feeling safe. Acceptance can be hard. It is learned early in life. We often see it in our parents and other people who have influenced our lives. We watch them respect and love the person that they are with no matter what. If you are like me and many others that I know, your family has what we call, 'an odd couple." The "odd couple," is that aunt who is the quiet, working class, who gives you her last; she is married to Uncle Joe, who is a nice guy, but who drinks a bit, is loud and often difficult to talk to. Like it or not, they have learned to accept each other (or at least tolerate each other). So, how does acceptance look in a relationship?

1. It sees the differences in one's partner and instead of putting them down, it seeks to

understand them and it tries to help them become better over a period of time.

2. Acceptance will look at the other person, see their differences and seek to determine if there is something that can be learned from that person. We are not talking about abuse. Abuse is different. No one should accept abuse on any level, but if your partner is different, there may be a few lessons and even growth opportunities staring you in your face.

3. Acceptance says, " I can see the challenges with this person, but I also see strength. I choose to focus on the strength while at the same time discussing the challenges."

Acceptance is one of those things that you have to be Christ-Centered to embrace. It takes patience, pure love, and the ability to avoid putting others down. You must be willing to try to help the person become better over time.

Chapter 6

Let's Put Some Fun In Your Marriage

We are of the opinion that one of the most overlooked things about marriage is that couples often forget to have fun. When was the last time that you and your partner laughed together? When was the last time that you did something really fun and relaxing? We don't presuppose that you are not doing that, we are simply reminding you that it is important and should be an ongoing part of your marriage.

We offer a few fun questions that you and your spouse can sit down and discuss. You will need to select a time when you and your husband/wife can give this some attention. Select a nice and peaceful area in your home. You can even prepare a nice cheese and cracker tray with your favorite beverage. In a relaxing tone, ask each other the following questions:

1 – WHAT IS YOUR FAVOURITE THING ABOUT BEING MARRIED?

2 – WHEN YOU WERE YOUNGER, WHAT DID YOU THINK MARRIAGE WOULD LOOK LIKE?

3 – WHAT WAS YOUR FAVOURITE PART OF OUR WEDDING DAY?

4 – WHAT IS YOUR FAVOURITE THING THAT I DO FOR YOU?

5 – HOW DO YOU SHOW ME THAT YOU LOVE ME?

6 – HOW DO I SHOW YOU THAT I LOVE YOU?

7 – IF WE HAD A WEEK ALONE TOGETHER, WHAT WOULD WE DO?

8 – LIST 5 THINGS YOU LOVE ABOUT ME AND WHY?

9 – WHAT IS MY MOST ANNOYING TRAIT? TREAD CAREFULLY! REMEMBER, THIS IS MEANT TO BE FUN! DON'T TAKE THIS TO HEART AND BE SURE TO LAUGH ABOUT IT TOGETHER.

10 – WHERE DO YOU SEE OUR MARRIAGE IN 5 YEARS? (10 YEARS? 20 YEARS?)

11 – IF WE COULD DO ANYTHING TOGETHER, WHAT WOULD IT BE?

12 – What Do You Value Most In Our Marriage?

Our values are so important, and it's okay if they are a little different.

13 – WHAT DO YOU FEEL YOUR NEEDS ARE IN OUR MARRIAGE?

14 – WHAT WAS YOUR PARENT'S MARRIAGE LIKE?

15 – WHAT EXCITES YOU THE MOST ABOUT OUR FUTURE?

Keep in mind that there are no right or wrong answers. The objective here is to seek to understand your partner better and to offer them the same. Be honest and open-minded as you speak and listen during this time. Keep it fun and enjoy this time together. All the best to you both!

Chapter 7

Acknowledging Your Partner and Their Needs

There is hardly a conversation about marriage that does not discuss the question of what really makes a marriage work. Without question, it offers many opinions, and the truth is, the answer is relative as we are concerned. All marriages are not the same and the dynamic of each depends on the two people who are involved.

On the other hand, some experts study questions such as those and often they come up with some answers that have merit. For example, there is one study that concludes that "turning toward each other," is the number 1 reason that marriages last. Is that true, maybe, maybe not? It does; however, deserve to be considered.

Just what does that mean? It means that couples often seek to get each other's attention but they don't always tell you exactly what they want. They say things in ways that suggest there is something more that they are after. Is that fair to you? Maybe, maybe not, that depends on who you ask. Should you have to be a psychic to understand your husband/wife's needs without them coming right out and stating them? We don't believe so, but believe it or not, it is important to know your partner well enough to be able to see beyond what they are saying.

To acknowledge a person means that you become engaging with them when they attempt to connect. For example, if you and your spouse are sitting at a dinner table and he/she is looking through their telephone and suddenly says, "This is interesting," what do you say?

Some people would say, "Nothing." Others might say, I would say, "Hmmmm." It is at this moment that the person is looking for acknowledgment and what they are expecting you to say is something like, "Tell me what you see that is interesting."

When you respond appropriately it helps to build affection and it reinforces to the other person that you are interested in what they are saying.

You have to make listening to your partner deliberately and intentionally. This may mean that you set aside time each day to simply listen to your spouse. You will be amazed at how much your spouse wants you to talk to them or respond to their simple thoughts or ideas.

Chapter 8

When You Have Had A Bad Moment With Your Partner

Marriage is about oness and it requires work, but in the process of "becoming one," you will find that often a disagreement here or there will happen. Some of them are worse than others, but from our perspective, disagreements don't have to be a bad thing and they can also help you to learn about your partner, help heal your partner, or even provide communication that leads to a more fulfilling marriage.

On the other hand, you must not miss the chance to make up because making up is the thing that will help you keep the marriage going.

Here are some things to consider when you make up:

WIFE OR HUSBAND MAD AT YOU

YOU DIDN'T MEAN TO HURT HIM/ HER, BUT YOU STILL HAVE TO MAKE IT RIGHT.

Relationships take a lot of work and at times they can be very difficult.

UCLA conducted a study on commitment in marriage. They studied 174 husbands and wives for their first 11 years of marriage to determine what they did to help make it through their times of conflict. They observed that the couples did three things that help them make it through conflicting times:

- They compromised during the conflict
- They were able to make sacrifices when engaged in conflict

- They continued to view themselves as a team

Disagreements are inevitable and those who feel they are not, miss the knowledge that disagreements do not mean the end of a relationship. The key is a matter of how you handle the disagreement. You can search the internet and read articles about marriages that ended, and you will be surprised at how many ended because the couple was not determined to work hard on resolving a simple (or sometimes, not so simple) issue.

On the other hand, the successful couple seemed to have focused on maintaining their relationship and doing their best to communicate with each other.

Since disagreements are likely to happen at some point, the ideal thing to do is to have a way to resolve them.

Here are seven things for you to consider doing when/if a disagreement arises:

1. Find out what's really going on

One of the first steps is to find out what just happened. To do this, you must give your partner a chance to talk about what happened and how they feel about it. There is no need to defend your position, you simply need to listen and seek to understand the problem as seen by him/her.

What is often missed is that most of the time, if someone is upset, there is a reason for it. You may feel that their reason for being upset makes no sense at all, and you have that right, but they also have a right to be hurt by what happened.

2. Give him/her some space, if needed

Everyone does not act or respond to issues in the same manner. Often, people may need time to think about what happened and time to think about how they will handle what happened before they are ready to discuss the issue. As a loving, caring, and concerned husband/wife, your job then, is to give them the space that they need to prepare for the conversation so that when it is approached, the right results are gained or at least have a better chance of being gained.

4. Talk the issue through and clarify

At this point in the relationship, you should be able to talk. The goal should not be to win, but to get clarity and to provide answers that may be needed.

5. Begin repairing the damage

At this point, apologies may be needed so that you can begin repairing what was torn down. In the process, make sure that your partner understands that you get their side of the issue and that you want to do everything possible to fix it and prevent it from occurring again.

6. Ask if there is something your /husband/wife needs from you

There may be something that your husband/wife wants from you that you may not be giving. Addressing this may help him/her understand the issue and prevent the issue from coming up again.

7. Talk about future steps

It may be a good idea at this point to talk about things that will help prevent the issue from being a problem in the future.

Chapter 9

Being Unequally Yoked

The word of God does not encourage marrying unequally yoked people. From a spiritual perspective that means that you are both on two different levels or understandings, practices, or beliefs when it comes to God. On the other hand, if you are married and one person gets saved or grows beyond the other person, you can survive even if your partner is not on the same page, Here are a few tips to help:

1. **Find a common authority in your marriage and build from there.**

If you want to determine if you are equally yoked or unequally yoked, find out who is the authority in the life of your partner. Providing that you are walking with

God, you can ask the person what their convictions are relating to how they govern their life. This should be done before you get married, but there is nothing wrong with having a conversation after marriage. There are so many questions that can be asked of each other that will tell you whether or not you are "equally yoked."

CHAPTER 10

The Step-Parent Issue

Often in marriage, two people become one, but in actuality, there is the factor of having children before you marry someone. If you have children before marriage, whether from a previous marriage or previous relationship, there is always the concern that the new mate will be able to get along with your children. Getting along with step-children (we like to say, "BONUS CHILDREN), can be difficult and when that happens it does affect the marriage. Sometimes it becomes too much to handle. Often one person or the other feels like they are in the middle. Either way, you have to be able to handle it. Here are some things to consider:

1. BE MINDFUL OF YOUR EXPECTATIONS

When you are considering blending families, remember that everyone has expectations. Unspoken or even spoken expectations can set you up for conflict. Your spouse/partner may expect you to discipline their child at times, but their child may not be accepting of that. Now you are caught in the middle. The opposite may also happen to you. You may be expecting your stepchild to understand that you have to discipline them from time to time and they may not be open to that. Sometimes expectations are not understood or even clearly stated.

Ask yourself these questions:

- Was the expectation realistic or fair?
- Did the other person have any idea you had that expectation?
- Is it an expectation you can let go of, or is it important enough to discuss as a family?

2. GIVE RESPECT…EVEN IF YOU DON'T ALWAYS RECEIVE IT

Giving someone respect when you are not receiving respect is hard to do. This doesn't necessarily mean you respect a behavior, it means you respect your stepchild as a person. It is recommended that you teach your stepchild a lesson in morals and values, by remaining respectful toward them. This requires patience. You must stick to your disciplinary processes and take the time to communicate clearly what is acceptable and what is not acceptable. This is necessary for both the smaller children and even the teens and adult children.

3. IDENTIFY YOUR INTENTIONS

Parents often have different intentions for the family unit. One parent may want the family to come together as a unit that includes all parties accepting this new living arrangement. The new husband or wife may just plain dislike that stepchild and have the intention, "He needs to get out of my house as soon as possible." The challenge here is that when that is the case it leads to a breakdown in the family dynamic and usually the family experiences chaos. This will almost always either destroy the family or certainly leave room for bad attitudes toward each other. We recommend that each person makes it clear as to what their intentions for the step-child(ren) are. We also recommend that if it gets to that point, the couple should get professional help.

4. REMEMBER WHY YOU'RE THERE

You don't always know what you are getting when it comes to step-children. On the surface, it can seem as if everything will be fine, but living with someone is different from standing outside looking in. The feeling of a step-parent feeling trapped after they have discovered that their step-child is disrespectful and difficult to live with is a very challenging position to be in. It is difficult for several reasons, but certainly, the fact that the husband and the wife are often divided due to that is one of the biggest ones. When this is the case, you must remember why you are there. Primarily you are there to love your spouse and to build a future with them. At some point, the children will be out of the house, but until that happens, you must manage this issue. We also recommend getting professional help for this one as well.

Chapter 11

Money and Your Marriage

Believe it or not, there are couples in this world who work together and become wealthy; but the bible's example of a couple who were once homeless but worked together to become financially independent.

You and your spouse can do the same. You have to concern yourself with ALL aspects of your life and be willing to discuss all of the possibilities that make you healthy, wealthy, and spiritually fit.

Let's talk about a biblical couple who worked together and came from poverty to wealth. Ladies and gentlemen, Aquila and Priscilla.

God's Blessed the Lives of Aquila and Priscilla

Perhaps we have a nice Jewish boy from Pontus, named Aquila who goes to Rome. He meets an aristocratic Christian woman, named Aquila and they get married and begin to establish their lives together in Rome. Emperor Claudius expels them from Rome which caused them to lose their home and their business.

Most people would have lost their minds and decided to move on in life without each other, but they did not. They still knew that they had each other and that God, in His wisdom, may have moved them to Corinth where they eventually met, ministered to, and eventually worked closely with the Apostle Paul in strategic missionary undertakings.

The Unity and "Two-getherness" of Aquila and Priscilla

When we read of Aquila and Priscilla they are always mentioned together, never separately. They were inseparable.

They opened their home up to the local church and they entertained traveling preachers This was a family business that they were both involved in. Third, instructing Apollos shows their intellectual intimacy. They both knew the Scriptures well and they wanted to share them with others. Finally, they put their lives on the line for Paul's sake, and moving for the sake of the gospel showed their crisis intimacy.

Aquila and Priscilla put the Lord first in their lives

The Apostle Paul describes Aquila and Priscilla as "fellow workers in Christ Jesus" (Rom. 16:3). They also were engaged in "secular" employment so that they were not a financial burden on the churches. Yet God blessed them with a very successful business so they could show hospitality to the saints by inviting the church into their homes.

These two are prime examples of what God can and will do for couples who seek Him and who love each other enough to stay together no matter what. You and your spouse must not only work on staying together but you must also work on becoming financially strong together. Find something that the two of you can do together that will bring in money. Work together so that you will not only be able to meet your financial obligations but so that you can leave a legacy for your family.

CHAPTER 12

The Importance of Marriage

If you are married, you may have discovered why marriage is so important and you may have experienced some of the good that comes from it. Or, maybe marriage was hard for some of you and you're no longer married. However, there is hope. But that hope starts with realizing that marriage can be more amazing than you have experienced or even thought.

Marriage eliminated loneliness for me and my wife. We are more effective in working as a team versus working as individuals. Through challenges, we have both matured. I believe God has created marriage to reveal more about Him and how awesome He is. And this is revealed through many of His purposes for marriage. Here are 5 reasons that explain the importance of marriage.

1. Beginning

"Marriage is more than a physical union; it is also a spiritual and emotional union." When you marry, you are beginning something that is designed, under the right circumstances to last forever.

Marriage is the beginning and is a life-long commitment to each other and to setting up a legacy for those who will come after you. It also provides an opportunity to grow in selflessness as you serve each other and your children. Marriage is also a spiritual union. This union mirrors the one between God and His Church.

2. Oneness

Marriage takes a man and a woman and starts them on the journey to " become one."

3. Purity

Marriage is designed for purity. That means that it demonstrates a commitment designed to remain pure and within the boundaries set by God for a man and a woman who have made a covenant of marriage with each other. We face temptation often in this life but purity is required from both the husband and the wife so that the marriage remains sacred. Purity does not remain pure without effort. Both parties have to be committed to keeping the marriage free from outside people of the opposite sex, gossip that tears away at the very fiber of the relationship, family members who may not agree with the union, and anything that threatens to destroy unity and commitment.

4. Parenting

When a marriage produces a child or receives a child as a result of an adoption, a spouse who had children before marriage, or if a family member has to live with one or the other spouse, it is an opportunity to expand the unity that exists. It can also be a test of the strength of the marriage, but two people working together can get through any test including parenting.

5. Love

Marriage is designed to mirror God's unconditional love for us. It is the kind of love that comes without conditions and it has no expiration date. It is a love that reveals itself not only through words but actions that demonstrate that it exists. It is a never-ending love that does not look for weakness but looks for opportunities to avail itself to its partner. The love that we are to have for our spouse the kind of love that allows us to provide, protect, and seek to help others to grow. Two people who seek to exhibit this kind of love will fulfill God's purpose and at the same time, the desire that the other person may have.

Chapter 13

Thinking About Getting Out of the Marriage?

Let's face it, people often think about getting out of a marriage! Before you do, let us give a few reasons to consider:

Stop trying to change your spouse.

One of the greatest temptations in marriage is the temptation to change your spouse into what and who you feel that they should be. Even if your spouse is noticeably in need of a change, you must let them make that decision for themselves. Trying to change a person rarely works out. Believe it or not, people have wanted to get out of a marriage because "He/she won't change." That is not a reason to get out of a marriage, especially if what or who you are seeking to change them into has nothing to do with how they treat you or how much that shows you that they love you.

2. Keep divorce off the table.

Often, when a marriage is challenged, one or the other person will bring up the idea of divorce. Usually, they don't want a divorce, they want to see if the other person cares enough to reassure them that divorce is not something that they want. Whether that is right or wrong, it does come up. The best thing though, is to never bring that up.

3. Seek out supportive people who will fight for your marriage.

There may come a time when marriage for you becomes too challenging and divorce seems like it is the best solution (and sometimes it is). We encourage you to seek every remedy first before you go to that point. If you are struggling in your marriage, one of the worst things to do is to share it with people who you may have the potential to enter into an emotional affair with. This is a person who may have feelings for you above being a friend. Instead, seek out people who exhibit that they want to see you and your spouse stay together. Those are the people who will help you stay rational and think through your challenges. These are the people who have nothing negative to say about your spouse, but who will encourage you to think things through

4. **Lean on the power of faith.**

There are times that amid your challenges, you can see a light at the end of the tunnel. It is during this time that you must put your faith to work and believe that things will change and that you will be able to work things out. It is during this time that you must focus on doing everything that you can to bring the marriage back to life. If it does not work out, you at least know that you tried.

Chapter 14

Has Your Spouse Changed

Has your husband or wife changed?

In most marriages, over time, people notice that changes in their partner occur. That is neither good nor bad, and depending on how you look at it, it could actually be cause for you to step up and be the woman/man of God that God ordained for you to be.	Marriage requires work, but more importantly, it requires patience and prayer.

If you are struggling with the idea that your partner changed, here are some things for you to consider:

1 Have you changed in a way?

Take a real good look at yourself to see if you have changed anything that might be a subject of concern for your spouse.

Looked at things from your spouse's perspective?

2. Consider whether or not your circumstances have changed

There are times when circumstances change and as a result, people may change. They may not change because they want to change, but because they need to put things into perspective. You must consider that as you evaluate your marriage.

3. Do the changes in your spouse create problems that affect your needs, desires, priorities or even your goals in life? Consider the fact that your spouse may not know that what they are doing is

affecting you in that way. Communication is key and you must take the time to share how you feel with them.

There are so many things to consider when you think about whether or not your spouse has changed. Most people spend their time worrying about how their spouse has changed instead of thinking about how they can manage the changes that the spouse has made. Think about what you can do to help your spouse understand how their changes have affected you and at the same time be fair and take a look at how you have changed and may be affecting them.

Contact Information

Email: theofficialpowercoupleinc@gmail.com

Website: www.theofficialpowercoupleinc.com

Amazon Books

Made in the USA
Columbia, SC
09 December 2024